What Our Readers Have Said...

"The Pinpoint Training Series delivers information that could be used in a lot different areas."

•

"Applicable and valid. The information is good."

•

"I like this because I can take them with me to read at a convenient time. I feel the little time I have to spend in the office is best use on activities that directly relate to revenue opportunities. I like the short amount of time it takes to keep up with these."

•

"I just read each book, and then file it for future reference."

•

"My thought is that the real value of these books comes into effect when doing the action plans."

•

"The challenge when I think a specific topic does not apply is to find a way to make it apply."

•

"Easy to use, understand, and reference if needed."

•

"Good layout and to the point."

•

"I think a lot of the recommendations in these books are very useful, and can be applicable to everyday situations. If nothing else, it's a good reference guide to fall back upon if a situation arises in the future."

•

"These books are relevant to today's work environment and the ongoing change in the way we manage our workforce."

•

"These books will pay for the time that I am investing. There are numerous good ideas that will streamline what I do and how I do it."

•

"All and all I think the Pinpoint series is a good program. I know other people I would love to have something like this. I think a lot of the suggestions are very useful, and can be applicable to everyday situations. If nothing else it's a good reference guide to fall back upon if a situation arises in the future."

•

"These books reinforce many concepts that I have learned through seminars, schooling and other programs. For myself, it serves as a constant learning tool that keeps me on top of the issues that many of us encounter every day."

•

"All in all, I think you have good training books. It helps everyone to review these materials, it serves as a good reminder to us on how to conduct ourselves."

•

"The information is valuable in these books."

•

"Good thoughts and ideas."

•

"I believe these books would be valuable to all employees."

•

Intelligent Decision Making

Pinpoint Management Skill Development Training Series

TIMOTHY F. BEDNARZ

MAJORIUM
BUSINESS PRESS

Pinpoint Management Skill Development Training Series
"Intelligent Decision Making"
Timothy F. Bednarz

Graphic design: Monika Pawlak

Majorium Business Press
2025 Main Street
Stevens Point, WI 54481
715.342.1018 • 800.654.4935

ISBN 978-1-882181-76-6

Printed in the United States of America

Introduction

The Pinpoint Management Skill Development Training Series is designed for targeted training and education regarding increased improvement in a specific skill or competency.

Each book within this series is designed to be easy to use, understand and apply to your job. It can be used as a basis for training individuals, as a discussion guide or as a personal training tool.

Each chapter within this book discusses a specific concept. When you have completed all eight chapters you should have a 360° perspective of the topic.

Additionally, each chapter is divided into specific sections:

- The first section provides you with an overview of the topic
- The Implications section discusses why the concept is important, and why it is important to learn and apply.
- The Strategies, Tips & Techniques to Apply section teaches how to use and apply the particular concept to your work.
- The Points to Ponder section gives you something to think about or to be discussed with a group setting. These are questions not meant to be immediately answered, but to be pondered over time.
- The Training Activity section provides you with the tools to transfer what you have learned to your job. It is designed to help create an action plan to effectively apply the concept.

Each of the topics in this series is time-tested and proven in the marketplace. They have been used by thousands of employees as training tools. Many of the users have commented that what made these books valuable, was the ability to refer to them when a problem surfaced. They indicated that they remembered reading about the exact problem. They referred back to these books and found an appropriate solution.

You will find them equally valuable as a resource in your professional development library.

Table of Contents

LEARNING OBJECTIVES:

- To identify and apply the elements and factors of the decision making process.
- To identify the critical factors and benefits of decision making, and the impact they have upon management.
- The implications and ramifications that either enhance or diminish individual decision making and its functions and process.
- To overcome the problems and pitfalls associated with decision making.
- To apply effective strategies to enhance individual decision making.
- To understand cause and effect relationships and their impact as a result of failing to properly apply the concepts and strategies of effective decision making.
- To analyze how the decision making process impacts the development process.
- To identify the expected results and outcomes of appropriate decision making.
- To apply strategies to effectively enhance one's decision making capabilities.

1

The Building Blocks of Effective Decision Making

Decision making is a cognitive process leading to the selection of a course of action among alternatives. Whether an action or opinion, every decision making process produces a final choice.

The decision making process begins when an action needs to be taken, but one doesn't know exactly what to do or where to begin. The reasoning process can be rational or irrational, with most decisions based on explicit or implied assumptions.

IMPLICATIONS — WHAT THIS MEANS TO YOU

Decision making is a major part of any business's' daily operations. To quickly and effectively move an organization forward and sustain internal loyalty and cohesion, employees need to share in its processes and outcomes. Every company is responsible for providing key information on new innovations, products and services, as well as potential courses of action, not only to external customers but also to its own people.

In order to bring about favorable outcomes, companies must operate using far-sighted and careful decision making based upon critical analysis and applied logic. The company that uses its employee resources to help make and implement wise decisions is doing far more than surviving: it is using sound management practices and thoughtful planning to compete far more aggressively.

STRATEGIES, TIPS & TECHNIQUES TO APPLY

Building Block One: Applying the Principles of Decision Making

Judiciously applying specific decision making principles will more often than not make the difference between taking effective or ineffective action. These principles help ensure that all involved stay focused on their specific work-related duties as well as the overall objective the company is pursuing.

When it comes to effective decision making, paying close attention to the organizational universe is not optional, but critical. The attributes contributing to good decisions can translate directly into tangible benefits when applied to the broader framework of business-related operations. Each decision made should serve as a learning experience, whether or not it proves wise.

How is an effective decision made? Maintaining an understanding of the basic role of one's organization can support thoughtful planning and processes for decision making objectives, which tend to justify the future course of the company.

There are 10 basic steps to follow when a decision has to be made. These include:

1. Identify the purpose of the decision. What exactly is the problem to be addressed and why does it need to be solved?
2. Gather information. What factors does the problem involve?
3. Identify principles with which to judge the alternatives. What standards and judgment criteria should the solution meet?
4. Brainstorm and list a wide variety of possible choices.
5. Generate as many likely solutions as possible.
6. Evaluate each choice in terms of its consequences, using predetermined standards and judgment criteria to determine the pros and cons of each alternative.

7. Settle upon the best alternative. This becomes much easier once the above steps have been undertaken.
8. Translate the decision into a specific action or plan of action steps.
9. Carefully execute the plan.
10. Evaluate the outcome of the decision and subsequent action steps. Within this process it is important to identify the lessons learned. This is an important step for further development of more effective decision making skills and judgment.

Building Block Two: Creating an Objectives Hierarchy

The first step in the process is to identify the purpose of the decision making effort: What is the problem and why does it need to be solved?

In order to achieve this end it is important to generate, record and display an objectives hierarchy by creating a list in outline format. (Software applications are also available that allow individuals or groups to create organizational charts that work well in generating visually appealing objectives hierarchies.)

In establishing an objectives hierarchy it is essential to gather as much information as possible to identify the factors involved in the problem. Objectives should flow from "Why?" at higher levels to "How?" at lower levels. Higher-level objectives tend to be broad, inclusive, and even ambiguous, lower-level objectives more specific, which are mapped to real or actual organizational and workplace attributes or characteristics.

The objectives hierarchy should be inclusive, representing a mix of stakeholder views, and not make value judgments in respect to one objective over another.

Building Block Three: Designing Alternatives

For each objective or group of objectives within the hierarchy, it is important to identify the types of actions that would yield the optimal effect.

When designing alternatives, various objectives should have been detailed and considered within the hierarchy. With enough specificity, some may be flagged for specific action or categorized as activity-driven.

Designing alternatives tends to occur in two phases: identifying the principles by which to judge the alternatives—i.e. the standards solutions should meet—and brainstorming, or listing actual potential solutions.

Nine Steps for Identifying Alternatives:

1. For each objective or group of objectives in the hierarchy, individuals identify the types of actions that would have the desired effect.
2. Causal pathways among identified variables are reviewed. How might favorable interventions occur in any of these pathways?
3. Two or more options for addressing each objective are defined. These may be different types of activities, different levels, strategies, or approaches for the same activity type, or modifications to ongoing related activities. If there is already a proposed action, the activities that comprise it are detailed in terms of how they align with the measured criteria in the objectives.
4. Specific actions are grouped into alternatives. If there are competing objectives (perhaps reflecting different stakeholder values), alternatives can be developed that favor different groupings of objectives. In other words, different balances are sought among objectives in each alternative.
5. Conversely, the same balance of objectives by different groupings of actions can be striven for.
6. If based on the effects analysis a revision of alternatives is needed, it is wise to look for simple adjustments first. If major revisions are needed, the objectives hierarchy and decision making model should be revisited to determine whether erroneous or inconsistent logic led to problems.
7. An open mind should be maintained, with preconceptions about what is the "best choice" not allowed to limit any or all solution options.
8. For each alternative, specifics as to how, where, what, and when actions will occur should be outlined. Here it is important to make detailed assumptions about each modeled action early and explicitly

in order to minimize confusion when placing this information into a structured decision making model.

9. Results are recorded and activities plotted on a decision making map where appropriate.

Building Block Four: Evaluating Each Choice

For each alternative, it is best to be as specific as possible in terms of how, where, what, and when actions will occur. An analysis of effects may suggest modification of one or more alternatives or the creation of additional alternatives. If the latter is the case it will be prudent to return to the first stage of the process.

It is important to apply standards and judgment criteria (a set of indicators) to determine the pros and cons of each alternative. When the best alternative is identified, a process overview of the selected option is conducted.

During this decision making and planning arena, it is important to make certain that an action or set of actions is specifically geared toward achieving the objectives identified.

Within the evaluation or overview stage, further details can come to light that can either be added to particular action steps or grouped into a different set of alternatives.

POINTS TO PONDER – SOMETHING TO THINK ABOUT

1. How does being flexible and having the ability to cope with uncertainties apply to effective decision making?
2. Do you feel good decision making requires sensitivity toward others and effective communicative skills? Why or why not?

TRAINING ACTIVITY — APPLICATION & ACTION PLAN

Apply the principles of good decision making to a problem that needs addressing.

1. Undertake the process of determining an objectives hierarchy.
2. Identify all possible solutions.
3. Brainstorm further alternatives.
4. Outline specific action steps.
5. Evaluate the solution selected and measure it against the objectives hierarchy.
6. Implement the selected course of action.

2

Implications of Decision Making

All individual differences in decision making must be taken into account in order to clearly understand the dynamics of the process. Attention must be paid to both the process itself and the specific techniques associated with individual personal approaches that work to establish assumptions, viewpoints and solutions.

In order for a company to generate and capitalize on workable solutions, methods, practices and processes, it must incorporate a workable decision making and problem solving process as well as specific techniques compatible with individual styles.

IMPLICATIONS — WHAT THIS MEANS TO YOU

Problem solving is a process that attempts to close the gap between a present situation and a desired goal, wherein implications of the problem stemming from known or unknown obstacles tend to block the goal itself and the path leading to its attainment.

In contrast, decision making is a process where one of two or more possible solutions is selected to reach a desired goal.

STRATEGIES, TIPS & TECHNIQUES TO APPLY

Most researchers describe problem solving/decision making processes as beginning with the perception of a gap and ending with the implementation and evaluation of a solution to fill that gap.

The steps taken in both problem solving and decision making are very similar. In fact, the terms are sometimes used interchangeably.

Most models of problem solving and decision making imply incorporating at least four phases. Each phase of the process includes specific steps to be completed before moving to the next and includes:

- An input phase in which a problem is perceived and an attempt is made to understand the situation;
- A processing phase in which alternatives are generated and evaluated and a solution is selected;
- An output phase that includes planning for and implementing the solution;
- A review phase in which the solution is evaluated and modifications are made, if necessary.

Decision Making: The Human Element

Reaching workable solutions through effective decision making requires considering individual differences throughout its various phases as well as its required mental processing function.

Although there are a variety of ways to consider individual differences relative to problem solving and decision making, it is important to address the various personality types and temperaments of all involved in the process.

- Some individuals may tend to be extraverted, and want to talk through their ideas in order to clarify them, where introverts will be more inclined to take time to think through and clarify their ideas before moving on.
- Those considered sensing decision makers will be more likely to pay attention to facts, details, and reality and will also tend to select standard solutions that have worked in the past.
- Those who rely on their intuition will most likely attend to the meaningfulness of the facts, their interrelationships, and the possibilities of future events stemming from these facts. These individuals usually

exhibit a tendency to develop new, original solutions rather than use what has worked previously.

- Avid thinkers will tend to rely upon logic and analysis in their decision making. They are likely to value objectivity and be impersonal in drawing conclusions. Solutions will need to make sense in terms of the facts, models, and/or principles that are under consideration.
- Deeper feeling individuals will be more likely to consider values and feelings as part of the decision making process. They will tend to be more subjective and will most likely reflect upon how their decisions could affect other people.
- Gravitating toward structure and organization, judging types will tend to seek closure in the decision making process. Some will seek higher levels of flexibility and adaptability, preferring that the process consider a variety of techniques while incorporating elements that enable adaptation to unforeseen changes and events.

Decision Making Technique Implications

It is not enough to describe how individuals differ in their approach to or use of a problem solving process. Specific techniques of attending to those differences must also be identified. Fortunately, a variety of problem solving techniques have been identified to accommodate individual preferences.

Some decision making techniques are geared toward individuals who tend to be more structured, linear, analytical and goal-oriented in their approach. Other more holistic techniques will be better suited to individuals who tend to be emotional, intuitive, creative, visual, and tactual/kinesthetic. It is important that techniques from both categories be selected and used when making decisions or solving a problem.

Individuals normally tend to use either reflection or inspiration during decision making and problem solving. However, research demonstrates that they are more successful in generating quality decisions when a moderate amount of both processes is used.

The following techniques focus more on logic and critical thinking, especially within the context of applying a scientific approach to reaching a decision or solving a problem:

Analysis – Combines identification of the components of a situation or problem with serious consideration of the relationships among its various parts.

Backward Planning – Related to the more general means-ends analysis, a goal-selection process identifies the mid-range and short-term conditions necessary to obtain the specified goal.

Categorizing/Classifying – Identifies and selects rules by which to group objects, problem-related components, causes and effects, events and ideas.

Challenging Assumptions – Implies incorporating a direct confrontation of ideas, opinions, or attitudes that have normally been accepted without questioning their purpose, reasoning or implications.

Evaluating/Judging – Incorporates a comparison to a given standard and requires making qualitative or quantitative judgments with regard to value or worth.

Inductive/Deductive Reasoning – An organized and logical development of rules or concepts taken from specific instances or from identified applications based on principles or propositions using generalization and inference.

Thinking Aloud – Involves verbalizing a problem and its solution while others listen for various errors in thinking, reasoning or understanding.

Plus-Minus-Interesting (PMI) – Incorporating the positive, negative, and stimulating or challenging aspects of an idea or alternative, this process typically relies on using a balanced grid with pluses and minuses applied to previously established criteria.

Task Analysis – An evaluation of the various skills and knowledge needed to perform a specific task.

The following techniques are geared to individuals who need to apply more creative, lateral, or divergent thinking when making decisions:

Brainstorming – Spontaneously generating as many ideas on a subject as possible. Ideas are not critiqued; the object of the process is to form fresh ideas from ones that have already been acknowledged and agreed to.

Imaging/Visualization – Creates a "mental picture" of the total problem as well as specific pictures in relationship to its various parts.

Incubation – Involves setting aside the problem for a certain time period, and doing something else to allow the mind to unconsciously consider it.

Devil's Advocate – Used as a bridge to a new idea, this technique entails making a statement to consider and challenge a premise or solution.

Random Word Technique – Involves randomly selecting a word from the dictionary and juxtaposing it with a problem statement, then brainstorming possible interconnections and relationships.

Synthesizing – Combines problem or issue-related elements into a new and original pattern of thinking, reasoning and decision making.

Values Clarification – Utilizes role-playing, simulations, self-analysis exercises, and/or structured controversy in an effort to gain a greater understanding of individual attitudes and beliefs.

POINTS TO PONDER – SOMETHING TO THINK ABOUT

1. Do you see a link between personality characteristics and decision making strategies? Explain.
2. Are there other implications within the decision making process that were not addressed within this lesson? If so, what are they?

TRAINING ACTIVITY — APPLICATION & ACTION PLAN

The benefits of decision making can be considered to fall into three major categories: general, organizational and individual.

1. Describe how decision making benefits can be used as an agent of change management.
2. Explain how decision making provides for the generation of both objective and subjective criteria that can be used to select and evaluate alternatives.
3. Describe how using decision making in a work group or organization allows individuals to understand a problem thoroughly before considering alternatives for it.
4. Detail how the use of the decision making process can lead to enhanced unity within a work group or organization.

3

Guidelines for Effective Decision Making

Much of what organizational managers, supervisors and empowered employees do is solve problems and make decisions. However, as problem solving or decision making often entails reacting to a newly erupted situation, problem or crisis, many fail to understand the differences between separate circumstances.

Most decision makers are continually stressed and "under the gun," and when they encounter a new problem, they tend to resort to a default decision that worked in the past. But by taking this course of action, it is easy to get mired in a cycle of solving the same problem over and over again without seeing any actual resolution.

IMPLICATIONS — WHAT THIS MEANS TO YOU

One needs to take an organized approach to decision making. Not all problems can be solved and decisions made by following typical rational approaches. However, the following seven basic guidelines should offer a solid starting point.

It is important not to become unsettled by or anxious over the extent of these guidelines: with practice, they will become second nature. They can then be expanded and enriched to suit one's personal needs and disposition.

STRATEGIES, TIPS & TECHNIQUES TO APPLY

When it comes to making decisions, it is best to look at a problem as an opportunity to bring about a positive outcome. In the course of the decision making process, it is often wise to substitute the word "opportunity" for "problem."

Defining the Problem

Defining a problem often poses the greatest challenge during the decision making process. Individuals tend to react to what they think the problem is rather than seeking to understand more about why they think it actually exists. To adequately define a problem one should gather substantial input from others, along with varying perspectives and points of view.

It is important not to automatically ask, "Who is causing the problem?" as this type of focus often results in nothing more than blaming. Effective decision makers instead maintain a focus on the issues that need addressing more than on the people involved.

With this in mind, the following question needs to be addressed: "What can be observed that leads me (us) to believe a problem exists?" To find the answer, it is important to identify and detail:

- Where something is happening
- How it is happening
- When it is happening
- With whom it is happening
- Why it is happening

Describing the Problem

The process begins with writing a complete sentence that describes the problem. To best describe the problem, a chart should be created with a header such as, "The following should be happening, but isn't" and another chart with a header such as, "The following is happening while _____ should be occurring."

It is essential to be as specific as possible when generating these written descriptions. It is also vital to include the various information gathered and detailed during the definition stage—i.e., what is happening, where, how, when, with whom, and why.

Defining More Complex Problems

If the problem still feels overwhelming, it is important to break it down by repeating the techniques of the previous stages until a complete, detailed description is generated. A list will typically be created that pinpoints several related problems rather than one specific problem.

It is always extremely important to verify a problem analysis by conferring with decision making peers or other appropriate individuals.

When it has been verified that several problems are interrelated, it is important to prioritize which should be addressed first. To prioritize effectually, one must keep in mind the difference between "urgent" and truly important and problems.

What are oftentimes considered urgent problems are nothing more than symptoms of larger, more overarching issues. For example, if a person continually has to respond to so-called urgent phone calls, the reality is that a more important problem exists, which is the need to design or implement a system that can screen, prioritize and direct incoming phone calls.

Understanding One's Role in the Decision Making Process

A decision maker's personal role in a problem can greatly influence how he or she views others' roles in the process. For example, if a decision maker is severely stressed, he or she will probably perceive that others involved are also stressed. Or, the effects of stress may cause a decision maker to resort to quickly blaming, criticizing, lecturing, demeaning or chastising others. In yet another example, if an individual tends to experience feelings of guilt about his or her role in the way a problem is assessed and addressed, that person will tend to ignore others' levels of accountability.

One's role in this process can also affect the way potential causes of the problem are perceived. The saying, "It's amazing how much most people fail to know about what they don't know" highlights the importance of getting input from others who are aware of the problem and directly affected by it.

It is often useful to collect input from individuals one at a time—at least as part of the initial course of action. Otherwise, during the decision making process, people will tend to be shy or inhibited when expressing their opinions and impressions about the causes of problems. All decision making members involved in problem resolution should therefore write down their personal opinions, as well as applicable statements they have heard from others.

Regarding possible performance issues that may be associated with a particular employee, it is often wise for decision makers to seek advice from peers or supervisors in order to verify personal impressions of the problem. It is again important for everyone involved with the difficulty to write out a personal description of the cause.

Identifying Alternatives to Resolve the Problem

At the point of identifying alternatives—unless the decision involves addressing a personal or employee performance issue—it is highly beneficial to keep others involved in the process.

To identify what type of approach to use to solve the issue or problem, it is best to begin by brainstorming likely solutions. This step includes collecting as many ideas as possible and screening or assessing them to find the best idea. It is vital not to pass any judgment on ideas: brainstorming requires that ideas simply be written down as they are suggested.

Next, an approach to resolving the problem should be selected. When selecting the best approach, it is important to decide which approach appears to be the most likely to solve the problem over the long-term and which one appears to be the most realistic for generating an appropriate short-term solution.

It is also important to determine whether enough resources are available for the solution. Are they affordable? Is there adequate time to implement the approach? In addition, the decision maker must determine the extent of risk associated with each alternative. This step in the process highlights why problem solving and decision making need to be well integrated.

Planning the Implementation of the Best Alternative

The stage at which the action plan is generated, the implementation strategy can be initially formulated by answering the following questions:

- What should the situation look like when the problem is solved?
- What are the individual steps that should be taken to implement the best alternative?
- Exactly what organizational systems or processes will be modified or changed because of the implemented decision? For example, a new policy, method or procedure might be needed. Here it is important to resist succumbing to a solution that will convey that certain individuals or departments are "simply going to be expected to try harder."
- How will it be determined whether the steps within the plan are being followed as expected? These details will indicate either the success or ineffectiveness of the plan.
- What specific resources will be needed in terms of people, money and facilities?
- How much time will be needed to fully implement the solution? It will be important to detail a schedule that includes start and stop times, as well as when certain indicators of success are expected to be observed.
- Who will be responsible for ensuring the plan's implementation?

Once the questions above are answered, it is imperative to communicate the plan to those who will be involved in its implementation. Decision makers will want to make certain that continuous observation and feedback is built in.

Monitoring Implementation of the Plan

Decision makers should monitor the indicators of success. They can clarify monitoring elements by asking themselves the following questions and responding to them objectively and thoroughly:

- Is what is expected from the indicators actually being observed?
- Will the plan be completed according to the determined schedule?

If the plan is not being followed as expected, the following important questions will likely surface and need to be addressed:

- Was the plan truly realistic?
- Are there sufficient resources to accomplish the plan on schedule?
- Should more priority be placed on various aspects of the plan?
- Should the plan be modified?

POINTS TO PONDER — SOMETHING TO THINK ABOUT

1. From a decision making standpoint, why is it more important to maintain a focus on the issues that need addressing rather than on the people who are involved in them?
2. Thinking back, have you made decisions or solved problems by hastily reacting to newly erupted situations, problems or crises? Did you have some type of decision making guidelines you relied on when this happened? Why or why not?

IMPLICATIONS — WHAT THIS MEANS TO YOU

Once a solution to a problem has been implemented, use the following criteria to determine if the problem has actually been resolved or not.

1. Begin the process by resuming normal operations within the organization while observing whether any changes are taking place over time.
2. Detail the answers to the following questions in writing:
    - What changes should be made to avoid this type of problem in the future?
    - What was learned from this decision making activity?
    - Include among other things the gaining of new knowledge,

understanding and/or skills.

3. Take time to highlight the success of the decision making experience and problem solving effort and what was learned as a result.
4. Share the results with managers, supervisors and peers.

4

Stages of Decision Making

In order to thoroughly identify, assess and select a "best choice" alternative from among a variety of potential solutions, it is essential to understand how to utilize the various stages of decision making in a manner that accommodates creative insight and thought.

IMPLICATIONS – WHAT THIS MEANS TO YOU

Decision making is most powerful when combined with logical, intuitive and creative mental processing. The stages used at specific points in the decision making and problem solving processes are well suited to group settings but are equally applicable to individual situations.

Tunnel vision is the biggest obstacle to problem identification during the decision making process. Tunnel vision often leads to artificial restrictions on the search for alternatives because it leads to a problem being defined too narrowly.

In order to prevent tunnel vision and maintain focus on the main problem, four decision making stages and their individual steps should be followed in the specific order outlined below. Careful execution of these stages will help generate the best solution for an existing problem.

STRATEGIES, TIPS & TECHNIQUES TO APPLY

The Contribution Stage

The goal of the contribution stage is to gain a better understanding of the existing problem and the specific circumstances surrounding it.

Before doing anything, the decision making group must identify the problem and state it clearly and concisely. The idea at this point is to understand and maintain a focus on the decision making or problem solving process and its purpose.

The identification of a problem consists of not only describing it accurately, precisely and in detail but also addressing the possible gaps that exist between current perceptions of the situation and desired outcomes.

The following are four typical gaps that indicate a decision has to be made soon:

- Something needs to be adjusted or corrected because a current method, procedure, action or practice is insufficient to produce the desired results.
- Something needs to be prevented because of a possible threat or negative influence.
- Something is appealing, engaging or interesting and needs to be acknowledged, received or accepted.
- Something needs to be provided because an element seems to be missing, ignored or unidentified.

Step One: Brainstorming

To initiate effective brainstorming, group members should either individually or collectively write down possible solutions to the problem at hand with all alternatives objectively considered. It is important to brainstorm extensively in order to expand and build upon the ideas generated.

Once the brainstorming session has run its course, the group can begin classifying, categorizing, and prioritizing issues surrounding the problem. The goal is to create a hierarchy of issues and factors based on how essential each is to achieving a particular solution.

Step Two: Criteria

During this step, the group develops the criteria to evaluate possible alternatives for resolving the problem or situation. It is important to categorize criteria as either "essential" for a successful solution or simply "desired."

When the criteria are being developed, the group should establish boundaries, acceptable alternatives and important values or feelings that need to be considered, as well as certain results that should be avoided.

Once ideas are generated, the criteria need to again be objectively considered. Important criteria should be categorized, with the group making a preliminary selection to be used throughout the process. It should be noted that these criteria will probably need to be modified as other important facts and information come to light.

Step Three: Fact Gathering

This step focuses on gathering information and facts that are relevant to making a decision. It is a critical component in clarifying the aforementioned perceived gaps.

Quality is more important than quantity when gathering information. Too much information can confuse and complicate the decision making process.

Brainstorming can again be used at this point. Facts should be classified and categorized so as to clarify the connection between various elements of information. The goal is to establish patterns and relationships among the facts.

All considered information must be analyzed in terms of the group's problem statement and evaluation criteria; any non-pertinent facts should be eliminated. Relevant information and associated patterns should be prioritized by applicability to the problem at hand, and additional facts collected later if necessary.

The Procedural Stage

The group must actively develop, evaluate, and select alternatives and solutions to solve the identified problem.

Step One: Development

It is important to create alternatives over the entire range of acceptable options outlined in the contribution stage. At this stage the process needs to be free, open, and unconcerned with feasibility. This activity should ensure that nonstandard and creative alternatives are generated. Once again, the brainstorming technique can be used effectively, allowing participants to quickly record and share results without partiality and to use the input to develop additional alternatives.

A number of brainstorming methods such as "challenging assumptions," the "random word technique," and "taking another's perspective" can be used to generate more creative alternatives. Alternatives that appear unworthy of further consideration need to be eliminated.

It is possible to categorize or classify alternatives and consider them as a group, but care should be taken not to create categories that are too complex, unmanageable or cumbersome. If the group shows dissatisfaction with the quantity or quality of alternatives under consideration, a break may be beneficial in order to renew the group and inject more objectivity and fresh insight into the process.

Step Two: Evaluate

A list of specific advantages, disadvantages, and interesting aspects for each alternative should be shared, discussed and recorded. After eliminating alternatives that are clearly outside the bounds and parameters of the stated criteria, these advantages and disadvantages should be considered in more detail.

An analysis of existing relationships among alternatives should also be completed, which can be done by asking, "Is an advantage of one a disadvantage for another?" At this point, serious consideration should be given to the relative importance of advantages and disadvantages.

Only those alternatives that the majority of the group considers to be relevant and correct should be given further consideration.

Step Three: Developing a Solution

For relatively simple problems, one alternative may clearly be the "best choice" solution. However, in more complex situations, combining several alternatives may be more effective. A distinct advantage of this process is that—if previous steps have been completed thoroughly and with attention to detail—selecting a solution becomes far less complicated.

Before completing this stage it is important to diagnose possible problems with the selected solution and determine the implications of these potential problems. This means asking the question, "What could go wrong and why?" When developing a solution, it is important to discuss the worst-case scenario that could come about if the solution is implemented.

The Implementation Stage

During this stage, a plan with which to put the selected solution into action is created. The plan must be highly detailed to allow for successful implementation.

Methods of evaluation must also be considered and developed. When developing a plan, the major phases of implementation are considered first, with steps necessary for each phase outlined. It is often helpful to construct a timeline and diagram the most important steps in the implementation process. "Backward planning" and task analysis techniques can be useful during this stage.

The plan should be implemented as carefully and completely as possible, with minor modifications often needed.

The Reflection Stage

The final decision making stage—reflection—is comprised of three steps.

Step One: Assess Implementation

Once initially undertaken, this step should be ongoing. The group needs to decide how to determine "completeness of implementation" prior to evaluating the implemented solution's effectiveness.

The fact that this step is often ignored or omitted is one of the main reasons decision making and problem solving processes fail: it often never becomes apparent that the selected solution is simply not being effectively implemented.

Step Two: Evaluate Solution's Effectiveness

It is particularly important to evaluate outcomes in light of the problem statement generated at the beginning of the process. Affective, cognitive and behavioral results should also be considered, especially if they have been identified as important criteria. The solution should be judged according to its overall efficiency and impact on the people involved.

Step Three: Modification

When necessary, the solution should be modified according to suggestions generated during the previous step, as evaluation often brings additional problems to light that will need to be considered and addressed by the group. Issues identified that focus on implementation efficiency and effectiveness should be targeted.

POINTS TO PONDER — SOMETHING TO THINK ABOUT

1. How do you see the stages of decision making benefiting your ability to manage change effectively?
2. Do you personally feel there is a need to develop and use a problem solving/decision making process that is both scientific and considerate of individual differences and viewpoints? Why or why not?

TRAINING ACTIVITY — APPLICATION & ACTION PLAN

The benefits associated with a rigorous model of decision making can be placed into two major categories: general and organizational. One of the primary benefits of using the process described in this lesson is that it is an effective way of managing change. Because rapid and unpredictable change is the norm today, it is important that sufficient resources be available to manage it.

Consider your own workplace. Create a list of four ways effective decision making impacts organizational change.

5

Three Models to Boost Decision Making Outcomes

Decision making is the process of arriving at a judgment that is based on the feedback of multiple individuals. It is a key component in the overall functioning of an organization, its creative power to transform itself, and its ability to refresh organizational performance.

Models promote the discovery and resolution of problems that occur during the decision making process.
Group decision making is essential to generating organizational change initiatives, innovation and creativity. Many types of models can serve as logical, organized, efficient tools to develop productive outcomes through collective knowledge gathering, analyzing, thinking and reasoning.

Using an effective model that meets the needs of a particular situation is key. An applicable model is necessary to promote the discovery and resolution of a problem and its related issues. It also aids in identifying creative alternatives that lead to a more innovative solution and outcome.

To enhance and boost innovation and creative outcomes within the decision making process, three separate models should be considered: the logic-driven model, the forced opinion model and the course of action model. Each carries distinct advantages and disadvantages that should be analyzed and addressed.

IMPLICATIONS — WHAT THIS MEANS TO YOU

In every organization, decisions of various size and importance have to be made daily. These decisions have ramifications in terms of both the resources involved in making and implementing them and the impact these decisions ultimately produce.

For example, a small-scale decision might account for the computers a specific department can purchase. Making this decision affects the resources of time and energy in regard to the particular computer users' need for speed, memory and other requirements. It also requires input from purchasing department representatives who actively research and give authorization to acquire the computers. The capability of these computers to meet users' particular requirements is what actually affects the outcome of the decision.

Large-scale decisions are often more involved and detailed. For example, deciding what level of service a company's customers require will tend to affect time and energy for many employees. Some decision making members will be responsible for researching consumer markets, while others will need to focus on gathering information on the company's current level of service and analyzing related customer satisfaction data. Still others will be in charge of developing and launching better customer service initiatives. Depending on the size of the organization, such decisions will often have the potential to make or break a company.

A group decision making model is best utilized when making logical and lower-risk judgments. It is also well suited to closing the gaps in innovative thinking in order to arrive at creative solution alternatives.

STRATEGIES, TIPS & TECHNIQUES TO APPLY

Below are detailed the three basic models that can be used with group decision making, each with its own unique structure, assumptions, effectiveness and criteria.

The Logic-Driven Model

The logic-driven model tends to be grounded in specific goals and objectives, alternatives, consequences and optimization. It is effective because of its simple structure, ease of use, and the fact that it tends to incorporate intuitive thought and creative, constructive reasoning.

The model assumes that complete information regarding the decision to be made is accessible and presented in order to yield an accurate identification of a given problem and its solution. It also assumes that decision makers will consistently assess the advantages and disadvantages in regard to pre-established goal and objective criteria of determined alternatives.

With group members typically evaluating the consequences of using or disregarding each alternative, the most significant advantage of applying this model is that it tends to follow a consistent, rational, sequenced structure. Decisions are made deductively by identifying and determining specific goals or objectives that need to be achieved and by using the solution that is most likely to achieve those ends.

Throughout the process, decision makers assess, appraise and evaluate potential alternatives based on the information they have at hand.

The logic-driven model does have one major disadvantage in that it assumes there are no innate biases in the decision making process. The reality is that individuals involved in the process do tend to bring their own perceptions, viewpoints, experiences and "baggage" with them. This is something that should be addressed upfront in the decision making process. Finding common ground and striving to reach consensus in terms of solutions and alternatives can help overcome biases.

The Forced Opinion Model

The forced opinion model centers on the preconceived ideas, agendas and concepts that decision makers bring to the process. In contrast to the logic-driven model, individuals involved do not make rational choices driven by specific goals and objectives; rather, the deciders tend to be motivated by their own personal needs and viewpoints.

The forced opinion model typically involves a cycle of bargaining among the involved decision makers, which is done for the sole purpose of getting one's personal perspective accepted and acted upon. This process involves individual decision makers trying to bend and persuade powerful people within the group to adopt their viewpoints.

With this model, full information is not made available to everyone, nor is "best choice" acceptance and positioning focused upon. Gathering and presenting all necessary information is highly unlikely since the model tends to operate on elements of manipulation and negotiation, which in turn are often influenced by power, special consideration and "string pulling."

Information is often withheld to better advance a given perspective. Since information is withheld and/or incomplete, ascertaining an optimal viewpoint is not a key concern when using this model. As group members involved in this type of decision making realm tend to have completely different agendas, they need to negotiate with each other and then present their cases to those who have the final say.

The chief advantage of this model is that it is representative of the subjective manner in which the real world often operates. It also ultimately minimizes conflict because it recognizes that individuals will always have personal biases and agendas that affect their behavior. By identifying and acknowledging this fact, potential problems and conflict can be predicted and subsequently minimized or negated.

There is also a downside to using this model: because of bargaining, maneuvering and actions that rely on withholding information, the best possible solution or decision is often not selected, leading to long-lasting negative or damaging effects.

Once group members discover that personal input and viable alternatives were ignored or rejected during the application of this model, many individuals end up feeling betrayed or angry: they resent the ploys, deception and pretexts that were built into the process.

If the forced opinion model is to be utilized, the decision making group must be made fully aware of its operation and structure upfront. In this way group members can be prepared with persuasive arguments and detailed information that will help shore up support for their positions and perspectives.

The Course of Action Model

In contrast to the forced opinion model, the course of action model, also often referred to as "the process model," is quite structured. Decisions made using this model are based upon standard operating procedures or pre-established organizational guidelines and standards. Actions and behaviors of group members are expected to conform to these standards. Past, present and future organizational events, experiences and projections are important under this model because they tend to be seen as reliable and steadfast foundations for the decision making process.

Traditionalism, harmony and conformity form the basis of this model. For the most part, conformity helps minimize elements of doubt, perceptive unreliability and lack of caution when the group is developing alternatives and solutions. Conformity also ensures each of these elements are dealt with appropriately and logically throughout the process. If decision makers are uncertain about the potential effectiveness or consequences of a decision, they can automatically default to the safety net of pre-established organizational standards and guidelines.

It should not be assumed that decisions made under this model are without solid reasoning or objectivity. This type of model usually provides a solid framework for identifying possible alternatives and a best choice selection.

When a group understands that it is working under a process model, the effectiveness of decision making tends to increase. An awareness that judgments are made relative to standard operating procedures enables individuals to anticipate potential obstacles involved with a decision. Individuals can research the pre-established guidelines that are applicable to certain problems and then adjust their discussions or points of view accordingly.

POINTS TO PONDER — SOMETHING TO THINK ABOUT

1. What type of model do you currently use when a decision needs to be made? Does it seem to work effectively? Why or why not?
2. In your own words, what does the phrase, "Decision making is the process of arriving at a judgment that is based upon participant feedback" mean?

TRAINING ACTIVITY — APPLICATION & ACTION PLAN

Evaluate your current decision making process before selecting another process or model to replace it. Use this analysis to gain valuable insight into the working dynamics of how decisions are made, as well as the group processes behind the decisions.

1. Begin by determining which model, if any, your group is currently using to make decisions.
2. Outline its structure and process.
3. Identify group members' rationale for judgment.
4. In order to enhance its usefulness or determine its actual ineffectiveness, address your current model's actual and potential problems.
5. Define what does and does not work in terms of the model's ability to produce potential alternatives and solution outcomes.
6. Determine what decision makers need to avoid when applying the process or model.
7. Facilitate a detailed list of needed improvements.
8. Assess and analyze the group's decision making interaction, intuition, communication and listening, as well as its flow of reasoning. Use this assessment to help formulate an enhanced or novel decision making process.

6

Analytical Thinking and Decision Making

It is essential to have a fundamental understanding of how analytical thinking works in the decision making process. A major part of any decision making process, analytical thinking:

- Identifies specific tools and techniques to apply during the decision making life cycle
- Creates a framework for managing a decision making issue, from its identification to its resolution

Analytical thinking is a five-step scientific process and approach to decision making and problem solving that includes:

- Defining the problem
- Testing the problem's hypothesis
- Focusing on facts
- Analyzing the problem by using various analytical tools
- Recommending a solution

IMPLICATIONS — WHAT THIS MEANS TO YOU

A problem is a situation that is judged as needing correction. It indicates that a state of wholeness is lacking within a particular situation or circumstance.

It is the job of decision makers to make sure they are solving or acting upon the right problem or issue, not necessarily the one initially presented to them.

From an analytical point of view, facing a problem begs two questions: What is it that truly needs to be decided upon? What action needs to be taken? Clearly defining a problem undoubtedly improves the decision maker's focus. It also tends to drive the analytical thinking process.

Problem defining is often discovery-driven. Concerned individuals directly affected by something lacking that they need to have in order to improve their circumstances, abilities or output will initially identify most problems.

The identification process then continues with a conceptual definition and a critical analysis process, which includes exploring the root cause, conducting an impact analysis, etc. The problem eventually becomes reshaped and redefined in terms of interrelated issues.

STRATEGIES, TIPS & TECHNIQUES TO APPLY

Formulating a Hypothesis

Analytical thinking is involved in formulating a hypothesis and attempting to prove or disprove it. A hypothesis can only be formulated after careful observation. Breaking down a problem into key drivers and root causes typically helps formulate a hypothesis. From there, specific ideas, concepts, reasoning and suppositions can be tested. The purpose of hypothesis formulation is to ascertain the validity of an idea through investigative efforts.

Analytical thinking, in conjunction with hypothesizing, lays out a roadmap for effectively and realistically approaching a problem in order to find a workable solution.

Collecting the Facts

Facts are considered to be meaningful data and information that have merit—in other words, they are not false or misleading. Factual information tends to be derived from expert opinion and is qualitative and quantitative in nature.

From an analytical point of view, facts must be measurable in terms of performance or results.

Gathering relevant data and information is a critical step in supporting the analysis required for proving or disproving a hypothesis.

Within an analytical thinking framework, gathering factual, usable information requires knowing:

- Where to "dig"
- How to filter through bits and pieces of collected information
- How to verify the data and information through past experiences
- How to apply the data and information as it relates to potential desirable solutions

Conducting an Analysis

Analysis is the deliberate process of breaking a problem down through the application of knowledge and other diagnostic and investigative techniques. An analysis of the facts is required to prove or disprove a hypothesis. It also provides an understanding of the major issues and drivers behind a problem.

It is generally better to spend more time analyzing than collecting data and information. The goal is to find the "gems" that can quickly confirm or disprove a hypothesis. Conducting a root cause analysis, a storyboarding exercise, and/or a force field analysis are just a few of the many analytical techniques that can be used to effectually test a hypothesis.

Developing the Solution

A solution is the final recommendation presented, and is based on the outcomes of the hypothesis testing process. As solutions are what make or break organizational initiatives, transitions and change, it is critical to ensure a solution is appropriate to the problems being addressed.

Solutions are useless if they cannot be implemented. Running an actual example through a solution is an effective way of testing its effectiveness and viability.

How Analytical Thinking Is Used in the Problem Identification Process

A problem becomes known when a person observes a discrepancy between the way things are and the way things ought to be. Problems can be generally identified by:

- Doing comparative and/or benchmarking examinations;
- Doing performance reporting, which consists of an assessment of current performance against goals and objectives;
- Doing a SWOT Analysis, which is an assessment of strengths, weaknesses, opportunities and threats;
- Analyzing complaints and the factors behind them;
- Reviewing surveys.

Getting to the Root of the Problem

From an analytical thinking perspective, a root cause is a specific underlying problem that can reasonably be identified and that decision making can control or remedy. It is important to remember that what is assumed to be a problem requiring remedial action is often not the real problem at all. Analytical thinking and reasoning is always required to get at the real causes of a particular problem; considerable probing is also often necessary.

Applying the following techniques is extremely helpful in identifying root causes:

> *The Five Why Technique* – Useful for quickly getting to the root cause of the problem, this technique requires decision makers to ask themselves five times why the problem exists.
>
> *Root Cause Analysis* – An effective method of probing, root cause analysis helps identify what, how and why something occurred. One way to conduct such an analysis is to create a cause and effect chart or diagram in order to categorize the potential sources of problems in an orderly way. Through analytical thinking and reasoning, the process unearths the heart of a problem.

Force Field Analysis – This technique visually illustrates the forces that work to impact a problem or issue.

Process Mapping – This technique charts the "as is" flow of activities that make up a process. It effectively identifies excessive handoffs, redundancies and other prime causes of inefficiencies.

Benchmarking – This approach measures existing performance against another internal or external source. It identifies several issues not otherwise revealed through the other techniques.

Common Decision Making Pitfalls

Once a problem is defined, decision makers must have the ability to develop a workable solution. If they have little or no authority to make recommendations as to how to handle a problem, then it is obviously outside the scope of the decision making project. In such situations, the initial definition of the problem may not be accurate.

Sometimes individuals involved in a decision making process lack knowledge and experience. Some problems can be unique and therefore require the involvement of more experienced decision makers to validate the problem and its possible solutions in relation to other sources (e.g., past projects, other experts, etc.).

At times, decisions makers will find that the best solutions to a problem are too difficult or complex to fully implement. As such, it is important to be aware of the full ramifications before recommending what appears to be the optimal solution.

It should always be remembered that most decision making efforts and their solutions will require some degree of compromise for implementation.

POINTS TO PONDER — SOMETHING TO THINK ABOUT

1. Have you ever rushed to collect information before you knew what facts and data to collect in regard to the decision making and/or problem solving techniques you planned to use? If so, what was the result?
2. Do you make it a point to test your solutions as much as you can? Why or why not?

TRAINING ACTIVITY — APPLICATION & ACTION PLAN

Applying tools and techniques for conducting an analysis is an integral part of the analytical decision making process. It helps one make sense of the information collected.

1. Define a problem or issue that requires a solution or decision be developed.
2. What things help to clearly define the issues surrounding the problem and solution?
3. Conduct an analysis by answering the following questions:
   - What are the most important issues to address?
   - What forces can influence the problem?
   - What are the core factors and influences related to the problem?
   - What areas are weak?
4. Finally, match the clearly defined questions and issues with the appropriate analytical tool to determine root causes and possible solutions.

7

Critical Thinking Is Essential for Effective Decision Making

Critical thinking is an essential aspect of the decision making process. Individuals who are critical thinkers analyze, consider and synthesize pieces of information and facts in order to apply them to generating appropriate alternatives that lead to effective solutions.

Much of everyone's thinking tends to be biased, imprecise, unclear, uninformed or prejudiced. As these are severely limiting attributes for decision makers, critical thinking is needed to improve the quality and value of their determinations.

When making decisions, critical thinking is essential for:

- Overcoming problems;
- Identifying changes, modifications or adaptations within work structures, methods and problem solving situations;
- Resolving situational conflict and urgent issues throughout the decision making process;
- Inventing and implementing new ideas, techniques and solutions for given problems or issues.

IMPLICATIONS – WHAT THIS MEANS TO YOU

Critical thinking development is a gradual process that requires mastering plateaus of learning as well as maintaining a serious focus on the process itself. It also requires changing personal habits of thought, which tends to be a long-term effort.

Within the realm of decision making, it is important to recognize what critical thinking is *not*:

- Saying something without carefully thinking it through;
- Taking a guess at what one thinks should be done;
- Utilizing nonfactual information or material to analyze, discuss or examine an issue;
- Doing something just because it has always been done;
- Believing something because it is what everyone else tends to believe;
- Arguing about something when there are no facts to back up the argument.

Critical thinkers possess certain qualities that enable them to make effective decisions. These individuals are typically "deep thinkers" who tend to:

- Be self-disciplined, directed, monitored and corrective thinkers;
- Clearly and precisely raise essential or crucial questions and problems;
- Gather, assemble, evaluate and appraise relevant information;
- Arrive at well-reasoned deductions, conclusions and solutions while measuring and testing them against relevant standards and criteria;
- Think open-mindedly within alternative systems of thought while continually recognizing and assessing their assumptions and lines of reasoning;
- Communicate effectively with others in seeking out and determining solutions for identified problems and challenges.

STRATEGIES, TIPS & TECHNIQUES TO APPLY

There are generally six developmental thinking phases that lead to one mastering the art of critical thinking. Through extensive practice and applications of the process, individuals can expect to begin changing their individual habits of thought, which will ultimately lead to more proficient decision making. Each progressive phase is described below.

> *Phase One: The Unenlightened Thinker* – These individuals are generally not unaware that significant problems exist within their thought processes.
>
> *Phase Two: The Confronted Thinker* – These people are aware of existing problems in their thought processes.
>
> *Phase Three: The Novice Thinker* – These individuals try to initiate improvements in their thinking—but without relying on regular or consistent practice.
>
> *Phase Four: The Proactive Thinker* – These people recognize the importance of regular practice in improving and enhancing their thinking.
>
> *Phase Five: The Developed Thinker* – These individuals begin to advance in accordance with the amount of practice they put into the process.
>
> *Phase Six: The Mastery Thinker* – Because these individuals are skilled, insightful and reflective, analytical and evaluative thinking becomes second nature for them.

Individuals will progress through these phases only if they accept the fact that there are serious problems with their current modes of thinking and they are able to embrace the challenge of changing. In addition, they must make it a point to begin regular practice to improve and enhance the elements of critical thinking.

Critical Thinking Relies on Clarity of Purpose

To develop critical thinking and use it effectively during a decision making process, individuals must be clear about the purpose of the problem or issue at hand and the key questions associated with it. To achieve this clarity, one must:

- Strive to be accurate, precise and relevant
- Practice thinking beneath the surface
- Be logical and fair-minded

- Apply critical thinking skills to all reading, writing, speaking and listening activities
- Apply these skills to all aspects of work and life in general

Questioning: The Impetus for Critical Thinking and Decision Making

Decision makers who lack critical thinking skills often end up being mere purveyors of others' questions and answers. They often initiate or respond to concerns or issues that surface spontaneously during a decision making discussion or meeting, but lack the background information that would help bring about deeper levels of evaluative questioning. Rather than questioning important problem-related methods, ideas or issues that need to be explored deeply in order to reach a decision on a solution, these individuals usually find themselves referencing others who are considered experts or leaders in their field.

When decision makers are not generators of in-depth questions and answers, they establish decision making environments void of critical thinking. Some even fail to seriously engage in thinking through or rethinking their own initiatives, issues, concerns or decision making concepts.

Critical Thinking Questions Keep Decision Making Alive

Decision making, in its truest sense, is effective only to the extent that fresh questions are generated and taken seriously. These questions are then used as the driving force for producing and implementing solutions.

To effectually parse any problem, decision makers must ask questions that stimulate deep thinking and force individuals to deal with complexity. Questions need to help formulate hypotheses, define tasks and problems, and identify issues. Questions of purpose, for instance, force individuals to define their decision making and problem solving task. Questions of information require decision makers to consider the quality of each source of information before accepting its validity.

Answers, on the other hand, often signal a full stop in thought. Only when answers generate further questions do they continue to add value to the decision making process.

It is important to remember that individuals in the decision making process who generate and ask serious and insightful questions are the ones who are truly thinking, developing and learning. It is possible, in fact, to move decision making forward just by collectively listing all of the questions pertaining to a problem, concern, issue or topic, including all questions generated from other questions.

POINTS TO PONDER — SOMETHING TO THINK ABOUT

1. How can you use questions as a driving force for generating and implementing decision making results and change?
2. If asked to identify the phase of critical thinking you currently occupy, which one would it be?

TRAINING ACTIVITY — APPLICATION & ACTION PLAN

There are two main questions that you should personally respond to when considering the critical thinking process in decision making. Answer these two questions and go over them with your manager, supervisor, peers, or an active discussion group:

1. How can I successfully become an avid critical thinker?
2. How can we as collective organizational decision makers help ourselves to practice better thinking in everyday work situations, as well as in day-to-day life?

8

Group Decision Making Techniques

There are several techniques and tools decision makers can use in order to make the best decisions possible with whatever information they have at hand. By applying these techniques and tools, it is possible to:

- Map out the likely consequences of decisions;
- Work out the importance of individual factors in terms of the decisions that need to be made;
- Choose the best overall course of action to take.

Decision making tools and techniques provide decision makers two main benefits. First, the tools give them a way to select among a variety of options. For instance, when a "go/no-go" decision is required or "decision paralysis" sets in and the need arises to get the process moving again, individuals have a qualified decision making method to turn to for assistance. Second, the tools help decision makers determine whether a course of action is worth following.

Good decision making techniques are based upon problem solving tools and the belief that decision making flows directly from one's understanding of the situation being assessed and evaluated. The techniques and tools detailed in this lesson are intended to actively facilitate this process. It is necessary to keep in mind, though, that tools and techniques are only meant to support one's intelligence and common sense—the two most important prerequisites for good decision making.

IMPLICATIONS – WHAT THIS MEANS TO YOU

Adaptable decision making tools and techniques provide superior documentation, rationale, collection and use of information, and interaction between decision makers. These attributes are extremely important, especially when generating and completing a decision alternative analysis.

Using good decision making tools and techniques can be likened to developing a protocol wherein a high-quality decision is based on:

- Accurately describing a problem and the criteria for solving it;
- Utilizing available information effectively;
- Collecting new information wisely;
- Generating and selecting from a wide range of alternative actions that are relevant to the problem;
- Distinguishing among facts, myths, values and unknowns;
- Describing consequences that are associated with alternative solutions to a problem.

STRATEGIES, TIPS & TECHNIQUES TO APPLY

The following two decision making tools can be used to effectively generate choices and solutions that are consistent with personal, organizational, stakeholder or other values that may be important to decision makers.

The Pareto Analysis

The Pareto analysis helps individuals make the most important changes during the decision making process. By conducting a Pareto analysis, decision makers are able to focus on a particular issue rather than spreading their efforts over the entire range of a problem.

The process centers on the Pareto principle, which states, "By doing 20% of the work, it is possible to generate 80% of the advantage of doing the entire job." Useful when multiple possible courses of action are facing a decision maker, Pareto analysis is a formal technique for finding the changes that will yield the most significant benefits.

Applying the Pareto Analysis

Decision makers conduct the analysis by:

- Listing the problems being faced or the options that are available;
- Grouping problems or options into general categories;
- Applying an appropriate score to each group;
- Working on the group with the highest score.

A Pareto analysis not only shows decision makers the most important problem to solve but also reveals how severe the problem is.

To begin the process, it is important to write out a list of changes that are possible to make. If a long list is generated, it is important to group them into related changes.

The next step requires scoring the items or groups. The scoring method used will depend on the type of problem to be solved or rectified. For example, if the decision maker wants to improve profitability, they would score each group on the basis of its profit potential. In another instance, if decisions and solutions are meant to improve elements of customer satisfaction, the groups might be scored on the basis of the number of complaints they would eliminate if implemented.

The first change to tackle is the group that has the highest score, as this will offer the biggest benefit if implemented. If several groups are being evaluated, the options with the lowest scores will probably not be worth implementing because fixing the associated problems may cost more than the solutions are worth.

The Six Thinking Hats

Decisions generated with the Six Thinking Hats® tool (Edward de Bono, *Six Thinking Hats*, ©1985 MICA Management Resources, Inc.) tend to be sound and flexible. Before any action is taken, the process helps avoid hidden decision making pitfalls and determine whether or not certain courses of action are feasible.

The Six Thinking Hats approach helps decision makers view important decisions from several alternatives and perspectives. It encourages better decisions by helping individuals transcend their normal modes of thinking, understand the full complexity of an issue and identify issues and opportunities that otherwise might not come to light. Too often, problems or issues are not addressed from emotional, intuitive, creative or negative viewpoints. As such, it becomes easy to underestimate elements of resistance to decision making plans and implementation procedures, as well as overlook contingency plans.

Applying the Six Thinking Hats Approach

Suited for individual use or in group settings, the Six Thinking Hats approach incorporates emotion, creativity and uncertainty into an otherwise exclusively rational decision making process. The technique also helps overcome factors of pessimism, which in turn allows for a more positive and creative decision making atmosphere. It blocks confrontations that tend to occur when people with different thinking styles need to discuss and assimilate the same information and frame the same issue or problem.

Each thinking hat is represented by a different color and denotes a separate way of thinking:

> *White Hat* thinking tends to focus exclusively on determining what can be learned from gathered data and information. Individuals using this method tend to look for and fill gaps in knowledge. It becomes important to analyze past trends and glean historical facts and/or data from them.
>
> *Red Hat* thinking is intuition-based and deals with problems by assessing related emotional implications and ramifications. The individual or group using this technique focuses on how other people may respond or react from a personal or emotional standpoint. Red hat thinking attempts to anticipate the responses of people who might not fully understand the rationale behind a decision or the situation, problem or issue that defines it.
>
> *Black Hat* thinking focuses on the negative factors and consequences

directly related to the outcome of a potential decision. The decision is carefully analyzed and assessed with a healthy sense of cynicism and skepticism. The object of the exercise is to predict why a decision might not work in order to highlight and improve upon weak or inappropriate points or strategies.

Black hat thinking helps make decision making plans stronger and more flexible. It helps identify risks and obstacles before a particular course of action is selected and implemented. It also allows people who tend to view things only in a positive light to see potential problems and challenges well before taking courses of action that may have seriously negative consequences. These individuals become better equipped to acknowledge and overcome difficulties and challenges.

Yellow Hat thinking is intended to help decision makers think more positively. It highlights optimistic viewpoints that help all involved see the benefits and value associated with a potential decision. It also helps the process move forward, especially when the situation is looking down, unproductive or complicated.

Green Hat thinking centers on creativity and encourages individuals to craft unique solutions for a problem. An unrestrictive and relaxed way of thinking, criticizing ideas, opinions and viewpoints is not considered appropriate or acceptable. The focus is on remaining open to fresh ideas and viewpoints.

Blue Hat thinking focuses on controlling the decision making process. The blue hat is typically reserved for those who facilitate decision making groups or meetings. These individuals direct the discussion with whatever type of thinking is appropriate for the moment. For example, when encountering difficulties or challenges due to a lack of ideas or creativity in the group, they direct activity using the green hat mode. Or, when contingency plans are needed, they typically encourage black hat thinking.

POINTS TO PONDER — SOMETHING TO THINK ABOUT

1. Have you personally used either one or both of the decision making tools detailed in this lesson? If so, where and when? If not, do you see any value in using either of them?
2. When thinking about the various thinking hats defined by Edward de Bono, which hat do you feel more comfortable wearing? Why?

TRAINING ACTIVITY — APPLICATION & ACTION PLAN

The decision making process requires procedures and steps. Consider the current state of decision making in your workplace, and then undertake the following steps:

1. Apply a Pareto analysis to focus on selecting the most important changes to make in order to initiate and implement the best procedures and steps for enhanced decision making within your unit, department or organization.
2. Apply the Six Thinking Hats technique to allow necessary emotion and skepticism to be brought into the open as part of a rational decision to change certain procedures and steps.

About the Author

Timothy F. Bednarz, Ph.D. is CEO of the American Management Development Group, Inc. For over 20 years he has researched, designed and authored hundreds of learning and development programs used by Fortune 1000 companies.

He is also the author of *Great! What Makes Leaders Great. What They Did, How They Did It and What You Can Learn from It* (2011).

Speaking Availability

Timothy F. Bednarz, Ph.D. is available for speaking engagements for your next meeting or association event. He can be contacted at 800-654-4935 or by e-mail at timothy.bednarz@majorium.com.

Bulk Sales

Bulk sales of this book or any other titles available from Majorium Business Press. Inquiries can be directed to sales@majorium.com, or by phone at 800-6654-4935.

Quick Order Form

Fax orders: 715-342-1118. Send this form.

Telephone orders: Call 800-654-4935 toll-free. Have your credit card ready.

Email orders: sales@majorium.com

Postal orders: Majorium Business Press, 2025 Main Street, Stevens Point, WI 54481, USA.

Please send the following books:

____

____

____

____

Please send more FREE information on:

☐ Catalog ☐ Speaking/Seminars ☐ Mailing Lists ☐ Consulting

Name: ____________________________________

Address: __________________________________

City: ____________________ State: _____ Zip: __________

Telephone: ________________________________

Email address: _____________________________

Sales tax: Please add 5.5% for products shipped to Wisconsin addresses.

Shipping by air:

United States: $4.00 for first book and $2.00 for each additional product.

International: $9.00 for first book; $5.00 for each additional product (estimate).

Made in the USA
Monee, IL
04 November 2026

67377564R00037